Table of Contents

Welcome to "Only the Essentials" — a unique collection of compact, no-nonsense guides designed to distil the core essence of complex subjects in a way that is both accessible and enriching. Whether you are a curious beginner eager to embark on a new intellectual adventure or a seasoned scholar looking for a clear and concise refresher, these guides are crafted to meet your needs.

In an age overflowing with information, it is often challenging to discern the fundamental truths amidst the noise. Our mission is to cut through the clutter and present you with the critical concepts, pivotal events, and key figures that define each topic. Each book in the "Only the Essentials" series serves as a solid foundation, planting the seeds of knowledge that will enable a deeper and fuller understanding to take root as you continue your journey.

Every guide is written with precision and clarity by experts in their fields, ensuring that the information is not only accurate but also engaging. We focus on delivering what truly matters — the quintessential ideas and insights without the extraneous details. By honing in on the essentials, we provide you with a streamlined experience that respects your time and intellectual curiosity.

"Only the Essentials" is designed for the modern reader: concise yet comprehensive, straightforward but never simplistic. Our books are perfect to carry with you, whether you are commuting, waiting for an appointment, or simply relaxing at home. They are your ideal companions for quick learning, thoughtful reflection, and stimulating conversation.

Join us in exploring the vast landscapes of human knowledge, from the profound mysteries of the universe to the intricate webs of historical events and philosophical thought. With "Only the Essentials", you will gain a robust understanding of a diverse array of subjects, empowering you to engage with the world in an informed and meaningful way.

Chapter 1: Introduction to Artificial Intelligence

What is AI?

Artificial Intelligence (AI) is the capability of a machine to imitate intelligent human behavior. The term itself is defined broadly as the endeavor to create computers or software that can engage in behaviors that humans consider intelligent. These activities can include reasoning, problem-solving, learning, understanding natural language, and perception. AI is a multifaceted field that lies at the intersection of computer science, neuroscience, psychology, and engineering.

At its core, AI aims to both understand cognitive processes and to build artefacts that exhibit these processes. This dual goal encompasses the theoretical exploration of what it means to think and be intelligent, as well as the practical application of this understanding in creating machines that can perform tasks requiring human-like intelligence.

The History of AI

The concept of artificial intelligence isn't new. Philosophers and scientists have pondered the nature of machines and intelligence for centuries. However, AI as a formalized field of study began in the mid-20th century. Here's a brief historical overview:

Early Foundations

- Antiquity and Imagination: Ancient myths and stories often mentioned mechanical beings endowed with intelligence or consciousness, such as the Greek myth of Talos, a giant automaton made of bronze.

- Mechanical Automatons: By the Renaissance, mechanical contraptions began to appear, such as Leonardo da Vinci's mechanical knight, which could perform some human-like motions.

The Birth of AI

- The Turing Test (1950): British mathematician Alan Turing is often considered the father of AI. His seminal paper, "Computing Machinery and Intelligence," questioned whether machines could think, leading to the creation of the Turing Test. This test measures a machine's ability to exhibit intelligent behavior equivalent to or indistinguishable from that of a human.

- Dartmouth Conference (1956): The term "Artificial Intelligence" was coined at this conference, organized by John McCarthy, Marvin Minsky, Nathaniel Rochester, and Claude Shannon. The conference is considered the birthplace of AI as an academic discipline.

Early Progress and Setbacks

- Early Optimism and Funding: Initial successes, such as the Logic Theorist and the General Problem Solver, led to optimism and significant investment. Researchers believed that machines would achieve human-level intelligence within a few decades.

- First AI Winter (1970s-1980s): Overestimations of AI potential led to disappointment as advancements stalled. Funding dried up, and the field faced significant setbacks during what is known as the "AI Winter."

The Rise of Machine Learning

- Expert Systems (1980s): AI shifted towards more pragmatic approaches, with expert systems like MYCIN showing that computers could be used to diagnose diseases and offer expert-level decisions in specific domains.

- Resurgence and the Second AI Winter: Despite the commercial success of expert systems, AI experienced another period of reduced funding and interest due to the high costs and limitations of rule-based systems.

Modern Era (2000s-Present)

- Big Data and Increased Computational Power: The availability of large datasets and advances in computing power revitalized AI research. Machine learning and deep learning became central to modern AI, leading to breakthroughs in various fields, from image and speech recognition to natural language processing.

- Deep Learning Revolution: Algorithms such as Convolutional Neural Networks (CNNs) and Recurrent Neural Networks (RNNs) achieved state-of-the-art performance in many tasks, reaffirming AI's potential and leading to widespread adoption in industries and consumer applications.

Types of AI: Narrow, General, and Superintelligent

Narrow AI (ANI)

Narrow AI, also known as Artificial Narrow Intelligence (ANI) or Weak AI, refers to AI systems designed and trained to perform specific tasks. These systems can outperform humans in their narrow domain but lack the ability to generalize or perform tasks outside of their scope.

- Examples:

- Virtual assistants like Siri, Alexa, and Google Assistant use natural language processing to understand and respond to user queries.

- Recommendation systems in e-commerce platforms suggesting products based on user behavior.

- Autonomous vehicles that can navigate and make driving decisions using sensors and machine learning.

General AI (AGI)

Artificial General Intelligence (AGI), or Strong AI, represents a machine with the ability to understand, learn, and apply knowledge across a wide range of tasks, exhibiting cognitive capabilities comparable to that of a human being. AGI remains a theoretical concept as of today, as existing AI systems have not yet achieved this level of generalization.

- Attributes of AGI:

- Flexibility in task execution, akin to human mental abilities.

- Ability to reason, plan for the future, and handle unanticipated situations.

- Learning from minimal data and transferring knowledge across different domains.

Superintelligent AI (ASI)

Artificial Superintelligence (ASI) is a hypothetical form of AI that surpasses human intelligence in all aspects, including creativity, problem-solving, and emotional intelligence. ASI could lead to transformative impacts on society, for better or worse.

- Speculations and Considerations:

- Existential Risks: Prominent figures like Stephen Hawking, Elon Musk, and Nick Bostrom have expressed concerns about the risks associated with ASI. Controlling and ensuring the safety of a superintelligent AI could pose significant challenges.

- Potential Benefits: If harnessed properly, ASI could solve complex problems such as climate change, disease eradication, and poverty reduction.

Conclusion

The field of Artificial Intelligence is vast and continuously evolving. It encompasses foundational theories, innovative algorithms, and practical applications that touch almost every aspect of our daily lives. From the visionary ideas of early pioneers to the current state-of-the-art technologies, AI stands as one of the most exciting and rapidly developing areas of scientific exploration.

In the chapters that follow, we will delve deeper into the fundamental concepts, core techniques, key technologies, and real-world applications of AI. We will also explore the ethical considerations, challenges, and the potential future impacts of this transformative field. With "Artificial Intelligence: Only the Essentials," our aim is to provide you with a clear and comprehensive understanding of AI, distilled to its core essence, and accessible for your learning, reflection, and stimulating discussions.

Stay curious, stay informed, and prepare to embark on an enlightening journey through the world of Artificial Intelligence.

Chapter 2: Fundamental Concepts

In this chapter, we will explore the foundational concepts that form the bedrock of Artificial Intelligence. These concepts not only provide the theoretical underpinnings of AI but also inform the practical algorithms and applications that have become integral to our daily lives. Understanding these fundamentals is crucial for anyone looking to delve deeper into AI, whether academically, professionally, or out of sheer curiosity. Our focus will encompass Machine Learning Basics, Neural Networks, Natural Language Processing, and Computer Vision.

Machine Learning Basics

Machine Learning (ML) is a subset of AI that involves the development of algorithms that enable computers to learn from and make decisions based on data. Unlike traditional programming, where explicit instructions are provided to complete a task, ML allows systems to improve their performance autonomously, adapting to new data without human intervention. Let's delve into the key concepts of Machine Learning:

Supervised Learning

Supervised learning is the most common type of Machine Learning. In this approach, the algorithm is trained on a labeled dataset, meaning that each training example is paired with an output label. The goal is for the algorithm to learn a mapping from inputs to outputs that can be used to predict the labels of new, unseen data.

Examples:

- Regression: Predicting numerical values, such as the price of a house given its features (size, location, number of bedrooms, etc.).

- Classification: Categorizing data into predefined classes, such as identifying whether an email is spam or not.

Unsupervised Learning

Unsupervised learning involves training algorithms on data without labeled responses. The goal is to identify underlying patterns or structures within the data. It is often used for exploratory data analysis.

Examples:

- Clustering: Grouping data points into clusters based on their similarities, such as customer segmentation in marketing.

- Dimensionality Reduction: Reducing the number of variables under consideration, such as Principal Component Analysis (PCA).

Reinforcement Learning

Reinforcement Learning (RL) involves training an agent to make decisions by rewarding it for desirable actions and penalizing it for undesirable ones. The agent learns by interacting with its environment and aims to maximize cumulative rewards.

Examples:

- Game Playing: Training AI to play games like chess or Go, where the agent learns strategies to win the game.

- Robotics: Teaching robots optimal ways to perform tasks, such as walking or grasping objects.

Neural Networks

Neural Networks are a class of algorithms modeled after the human brain's structure, designed to recognize patterns, make decisions, and improve performance through learning. They are the cornerstone of deep learning and have enabled numerous breakthroughs in AI.

Basic Structure

A neural network consists of layers of interconnected nodes, or neurons, each performing a simple computation. These layers can be broadly categorized into three types:

- Input Layer: Receives the raw data.

- Hidden Layers: Perform intermediate computations and transformations.

- Output Layer: Produces the final output.

Each connection between neurons has an associated weight that is adjusted during training. The training process involves forward propagation of inputs through the network and backpropagation of errors to update weights, minimizing the difference between predicted and actual outputs.

Activation Functions

Activation functions introduce non-linearity into the network, allowing it to model complex relationships between inputs and outputs. Common activation functions include:

- Sigmoid: Outputs values between 0 and 1, useful for binary classification.

- Tanh: Outputs values between -1 and 1, often used in hidden layers to center the data.

- ReLU (Rectified Linear Unit): Outputs the input directly if positive, otherwise zero, commonly used due to its efficiency in training deep networks.

Types of Neural Networks

- Feedforward Neural Networks (FNNs): The simplest type, where connections between the nodes do not form cycles. They are effective for tasks like image recognition and regression.

- Convolutional Neural Networks (CNNs): Specialized for processing grid-structured data such as images. They use convolutional layers to detect spatial patterns and are widely used in image and video analysis.

- Recurrent Neural Networks (RNNs): Designed for sequential data, such as time series or natural language. They have connections that form cycles, allowing information to persist across time steps. Variants like Long Short-Term Memory (LSTM) networks address the issue of long-term dependencies.

- Generative Adversarial Networks (GANs): Consist of two networks, a generator and a discriminator, that are trained simultaneously in a game-theoretic framework. GANs are capable of generating realistic data, such as images and text.

Natural Language Processing

Natural Language Processing (NLP) is a field of AI focused on the interaction between computers and human language. It involves enabling machines to read, understand, and generate language in a way that is both meaningful and useful.

Key Concepts

- Tokenization: The process of splitting text into smaller units, or tokens, such as words or subwords.

- Part-of-Speech Tagging: Assigning grammatical tags (nouns, verbs, adjectives, etc.) to each token in a sentence.

- Named Entity Recognition (NER): Identifying and classifying proper names, such as people, organizations, and locations, within text.

- Parsing: Analyzing the syntax of sentences to understand their structure and grammatical relationships.

- Word Embeddings: Representing words as dense vectors in a continuous vector space. Techniques like Word2Vec and GloVe allow for capturing semantic relationships between words.

NLP Tasks and Applications

- Text Classification: Categorizing text into predefined categories, such as spam detection, sentiment analysis, and topic classification.

- Machine Translation: Translating text from one language to another, a task embodied by systems like Google Translate.

- Question Answering: Building systems that can answer questions posed in natural language, used in virtual assistants and customer support automation.

- Summarization: Automatically generating concise summaries of longer texts, useful for news aggregation and document analysis.

Modern NLP Techniques

- Transformer Models: Introduced by the seminal paper "Attention is All You Need," transformers have revolutionized NLP. They rely on self-attention mechanisms to capture relationships between words in a sentence, leading to more effective contextual understanding.

- Pre-trained Models: Models such as BERT (Bidirectional Encoder Representations from Transformers) and GPT (Generative Pre-trained Transformer) have been pre-trained on vast amounts of text data and fine-tuned for specific tasks. They have significantly advanced the state of the art in various NLP applications.

Computer Vision

Computer Vision is an area of AI that enables machines to interpret and understand the visual world. It involves processing and analyzing images and videos to extract meaningful information.

Key Components

- Image Processing: Enhancing and manipulating images to improve their quality or extract important features. Techniques include filtering, edge detection, and contrast adjustment.

- Feature Extraction: Identifying important patterns and structures in images, such as edges, textures, and shapes. Features are used to represent images in a more meaningful and compact form.

- Object Detection and Recognition: Locating and identifying objects within an image. While object detection focuses on finding the objects' locations, object recognition involves classifying them into predefined categories.

Key Computer Vision Tasks

- Image Classification: Assigning a label to an entire image based on its content, such as determining whether an image contains a cat or a dog.

- Object Detection: Identifying and locating multiple objects within an image, often represented by bounding boxes around the detected objects.

- Segmentation: Dividing an image into meaningful regions or segments, such as delineating each object in an image with precise boundaries. Semantic segmentation involves labeling each pixel with a class, while instance segmentation differentiates between individual instances of objects.

- Face Recognition: Identifying or verifying individuals based on their facial features. It involves detecting faces in images, extracting unique facial representations, and comparing them to known faces.

- Motion Analysis: Analyzing and understanding movement within a sequence of images or video frames. Applications include activity recognition, gesture recognition, and tracking.

Techniques and Algorithms

- Convolutional Neural Networks (CNNs): CNNs have become the de facto standard for computer vision tasks due to their ability to automatically learn hierarchical features from images. They consist of convolutional layers, pooling layers, and fully connected layers.

- Pre-trained Models: Pre-trained models, such as VGG, ResNet, and YOLO, have been trained on large datasets like ImageNet and can be fine-tuned for specific tasks. They provide a good starting point and leverage transfer learning to improve performance.

- Data Augmentation: To improve the robustness and generalization of computer vision models, data augmentation techniques are applied. These techniques involve creating variations of training images by applying transformations like rotation, scaling, cropping, and flipping.

Applications of Computer Vision

- Medical Imaging: Assisting in the diagnosis of diseases by analyzing medical images like X-rays, MRIs, and CT scans. Computer Vision techniques help detect abnormalities, segment organs, and quantify measurements.

- Autonomous Vehicles: Enabling self-driving cars to perceive and understand their surroundings by detecting objects, recognizing traffic signs, and analyzing road conditions.

- Retail and E-commerce: Enhancing customer experiences through visual search, recommendation systems, and virtual try-on. Computer vision algorithms can automatically tag and categorize products, improving search accuracy.

- Surveillance and Security: Monitoring and detecting suspicious activities in real-time using video surveillance systems. Applications include facial recognition for access control, anomaly detection, and crowd monitoring.

Conclusion

This chapter has covered the fundamental concepts that are the building blocks of Artificial Intelligence. From the basics of Machine Learning, including supervised, unsupervised, and reinforcement learning, to the intricacies of Neural Networks and their various types, we have laid a solid foundation for understanding AI.

We explored the fascinating field of Natural Language Processing, discussing key tasks and modern techniques like transformers and pre-trained models. Additionally, we delved into Computer Vision, highlighting its core components, key tasks, and applications that have transformed industries ranging from healthcare to autonomous vehicles.

These fundamental concepts provide a strong basis for further exploration into more advanced topics and practical applications of AI. In the subsequent chapters, we will delve deeper into core techniques and algorithms, key technologies and tools, as well as real-world applications, ethical considerations, and the future of AI. With this knowledge, you are well-equipped to embark on your journey into the exciting realm of Artificial Intelligence, armed with a comprehensive understanding of its essential foundations.

Chapter 3: Core Techniques and Algorithms

In the journey to understand and harness the power of artificial intelligence (AI), it's essential to delve into the core techniques and algorithms that form the backbone of this transformative technology. This chapter will cover the primary methods and algorithms used in AI, including supervised learning, unsupervised learning, reinforcement learning, and deep learning. Each of these techniques has distinct approaches, applications, and implications, which we will explore in depth.

Supervised Learning

Introduction to Supervised Learning

Supervised learning is a type of machine learning in which an algorithm is trained on labeled data. Labeled data means that each training example is paired with an output label. The objective of the supervised learning model is to learn a mapping from inputs to outputs and predict the correct output for any new input data.

- Examples of Labeled Data:

- Images of animals labeled with their respective species.

- Medical data labeled with diagnoses.

- Customer transaction data labeled as fraud or not fraud.

Algorithms in Supervised Learning

Linear Regression

Linear regression is one of the simplest and most commonly used algorithms. It models the relationship between a dependent variable and one (simple linear regression) or more (multiple linear regression) independent variables by fitting a linear equation to observed data.

- Mathematical Model: $y = \beta_0 + \beta_1 x_1 + \beta_2 x_2 + \dots + \beta_n x_n + \epsilon$

- y: Dependent variable.

- β_0: Intercept.

- $\beta_1, \beta_2, \dots, \beta_n$: Coefficients of the independent variables.

- $x_1, x_2, \dots, x_n$: Independent variables.

- ϵ: Error term.

Logistic Regression

Logistic regression, despite its name, is used for binary classification problems. It models the probability that the dependent variable belongs to a particular category.

- Mathematical Model: $P(Y=1|X=x) = \frac{1}{1 + e^{-(\beta_0 + \beta_1 x_1 + \dots + \beta_n x_n)}}$

- The logistic function (sigmoid function) maps any real-valued number into the range (0, 1).

Decision Trees

Decision trees split the data into subsets based on the value of input features, forming a tree-like model. Each internal node of the tree represents a decision rule, and each leaf node represents an outcome.

- Advantages: Easy to interpret and visualize.

- Disadvantages: Prone to overfitting, particularly with complex trees.

Support Vector Machines are powerful for both classification and regression tasks. SVMs operate by finding the hyperplane that best separates the different classes in the feature space.

- Kernel Trick: SVMs can use the kernel trick to transform data that is not linearly separable into a higher-dimensional space where it can be separated.

Applications of Supervised Learning

- Spam Detection: Classifying emails as spam or not spam.

- Image Recognition: Identifying objects within an image, such as faces or pets.

- Medical Diagnosis: Predictive models to diagnose diseases based on patient data.

Unsupervised Learning

Introduction to Unsupervised Learning

Unsupervised learning deals with unlabeled data. The goal is to model the underlying structure or distribution in the data to learn more about it. Unlike supervised learning, there are no correct output labels to guide the learning process.

Algorithms in Unsupervised Learning

Clustering

Clustering involves grouping a set of objects in such a way that objects in the same group (clusters) are more similar to each other than to those in other groups.

- K-Means Clustering:

- Algorithm:

1. Initialize k centroids randomly.

2. Assign each data point to the nearest centroid.

3. Update centroids by computing the mean of all points assigned to each cluster.

4. Repeat steps 2 and 3 until convergence.

- Challenges: Choosing the number of clusters (k) and sensitivity to initial centroid placement.

- Hierarchical Clustering:

- Builds a tree of clusters by either a bottom-up approach (agglomerative) or a top-down approach (divisive).

- Agglomerative: Start with each data point as a single cluster and merge the closest pairs iteratively.

- Divisive: Start with all data points in a single cluster and recursively split the least similar cluster.

Dimensionality Reduction

Dimensionality reduction techniques are used to reduce the number of input variables in a dataset, which can improve the performance of machine learning models.

- Principal Component Analysis (PCA):

- PCA transforms the data into a new coordinate system where the greatest variance by any projection of the data comes to lie on the first principal component, the second greatest variance on the second principal component, and so on.

- t-Distributed Stochastic Neighbor Embedding (t-SNE):

- t-SNE is particularly useful for the visualization of high-dimensional data. It reduces the dimensionality in such a way that similar objects stay close together and dissimilar objects are modeled far apart.

Applications of Unsupervised Learning

- Market Basket Analysis: Discovering association rules that show how products are frequently purchased together.

- Customer Segmentation: Identifying distinct groups of customers based on purchasing behavior.

- Anomaly Detection: Identifying unusual patterns in data that do not conform to expected behavior.

Reinforcement Learning

Introduction to Reinforcement Learning

Reinforcement learning (RL) is a type of machine learning where an agent learns to make decisions by performing actions in an environment to maximize some notion of cumulative reward.

Key Concepts in Reinforcement Learning

- Agent: The learner or decision maker.

- Environment: Everything the agent interacts with.

- State: A representation of the current situation of the agent.

- Action: Choices made by the agent that affect the state.

- Reward: Feedback from the environment to evaluate the action taken by the agent.

- Policy: A strategy used by the agent to determine the next action based on the current state.

- Value Function: A prediction of future rewards used to evaluate the desirability of states.

- Q-Learning: A popular RL algorithm that learns the value of the action in a particular state.

Algorithms in Reinforcement Learning

Q-Learning

Q-Learning is an off-policy RL algorithm that seeks to find the best action to take given the current state. It updates the Q-values based on the cumulative expected future rewards.

- Update Rule:

$$ Q(s, a) \leftarrow Q(s, a) + \alpha [r + \gamma \max_{a'} Q(s', a') - Q(s, a)] $$

- α: Learning rate.

- γ: Discount factor.

- r: Reward received after taking action a in state s.

- s': New state after action a.

- $\max_{a'} Q(s', a')$: Maximum estimated future reward given the new state s' and all possible actions a'.

Deep Q-Networks (DQN)

Deep Q-Networks combine Q-learning with deep neural networks. A neural network is used to approximate the Q-values, allowing the algorithm to handle high-dimensional state spaces.

- Experience Replay: Stores agent's experiences at each time step in a replay memory and uses random samples from the memory to train the network.

- Fixed Q-Target Networks: Uses a separate target network to stabilize the training by periodically copying the weights of the primary Q-network.

Applications of Reinforcement Learning

- Game Playing: RL algorithms have achieved superhuman performance in games like Go, Chess, and video games.

- Robotics: Autonomous robots that learn to navigate and perform tasks through trial and error.

- Resource Management: Optimizing the allocation of resources in real-time, such as energy distribution in smart grids.

Deep Learning

Introduction to Deep Learning

Deep learning is a subset of machine learning that uses neural networks with many layers (hence "deep") to model complex patterns in data. Deep learning has revolutionized the field of AI, especially in tasks involving high-dimensional data such as images, audio, and text.

Neural Networks

A neural network consists of interconnected layers of nodes (neurons), where each node represents a function that transforms the input data in some way.

Structure of Neural Networks

- Input Layer: The initial layer that receives the input data.

- Hidden Layers: Intermediate layers that perform computations and learn to extract relevant features from the data.

- Output Layer: The final layer that produces the output prediction.

- Feedforward Neural Networks: The simplest type of neural network where connections between the nodes do not form cycles. Information flows in one direction, from input to output.

- Convolutional Neural Networks (CNNs): Designed specifically for processing structured grid data like images. They use convolutional layers to automatically and adaptively learn spatial hierarchies of features.

- Components:

- Convolutional Layers: Apply convolutional filters to the input.

- Pooling Layers: Down-sample the spatial dimensions to reduce computational load.

- Fully Connected Layers: Connect every neuron in one layer to every neuron in another layer.

- Recurrent Neural Networks (RNNs): Suitable for sequential data as they maintain a hidden state that captures information about previous elements in the sequence.

- Variants:

- Long Short-Term Memory (LSTM): Designed to overcome the limitations of vanilla RNNs in learning long-term dependencies.

- Gated Recurrent Unit (GRU): A simpler alternative to LSTM with similar performance.

- Transformers: State-of-the-art models for sequence-to-sequence tasks. They use self-attention mechanisms to weigh the importance of different elements in the sequence.

- Components:

- Encoder-Decoder Architecture: The encoder processes the input sequence, while the decoder generates the output sequence.

- Self-Attention Mechanism: Calculates the importance of each element in a sequence relative to others, allowing the model to focus on relevant parts.

Training Deep Neural Networks

Backpropagation

Backpropagation is a supervised learning algorithm used for training neural networks. It calculates the gradient of the loss function with respect to each weight by the chain rule, allowing the optimization algorithm to update the weights.

Optimization Algorithms

- Stochastic Gradient Descent (SGD): Updates weights incrementally, using one or a few training examples at a time, which allows for faster convergence and can escape local minima.

- Adam: An adaptive learning rate method that combines the advantages of two other extensions of SGD, namely AdaGrad and RMSProp. It computes individual adaptive learning rates for different parameters.

Regularization Techniques

- Dropout: Randomly drops a subset of neurons during training to prevent overfitting and improve generalization.

- Batch Normalization: Normalizes the input of each layer to stabilize and accelerate training.

Applications of Deep Learning

- Computer Vision: Image classification, object detection, image segmentation, and style transfer.

- Natural Language Processing (NLP): Machine translation, sentiment analysis, text summarization, and chatbots.

- Speech Recognition: Converting spoken language into text with high accuracy, used in virtual assistants and transcription services.

- Generative Models: Creating new data similar to existing data, such as Generative Adversarial Networks (GANs) for generating realistic images and text.

Conclusion

Understanding the core techniques and algorithms in artificial intelligence is crucial for leveraging the power of AI systems. From supervised learning's ability to predict outcomes based on labeled data to unsupervised learning's capacity to uncover hidden patterns, each technique offers unique capabilities and applications. Reinforcement learning empowers agents to make decisions that maximize cumulative rewards, and deep learning enables the modeling of complex patterns in high-dimensional data.

In the following chapters, we will explore key technologies and tools, practical applications, and the ethical considerations of AI. By comprehending the fundamental principles and methods discussed in this chapter, you will be well-equipped to navigate and contribute to the rapidly evolving field of artificial intelligence.

Chapter 4: Key Technologies and Tools

Artificial Intelligence (AI) has grown exponentially due to advancements in various technologies and tools that facilitate its development and deployment. This chapter will explore the most important technologies and tools that drive the field of AI, covering programming languages, frameworks, libraries, and best practices for data preparation and preprocessing.

Commonly Used Programming Languages

Several programming languages are frequently used in AI development due to their ease of use, support for machine learning libraries, and community support. Here, we provide an overview of the most popular languages in the AI domain.

Python

Python is undoubtedly the most popular programming language for AI and machine learning. Its simplicity and readability make it accessible for beginners, while its extensive library ecosystem provides powerful tools for experienced developers.

- Libraries and Frameworks: TensorFlow, PyTorch, scikit-learn, Keras, NLTK, OpenCV

- Advantages:

- Readability and simplicity

- Extensive libraries and frameworks

- Strong community support

- Versatility for different types of AI applications

R

R is a programming language and software environment primarily used for statistical computing and graphics. It is popular among data scientists for data analysis and visualization, and it has capabilities for machine learning.

- Libraries and Frameworks: caret, randomForest, e1071, nnet, tm

- Advantages:

- Powerful data analysis and visualization tools

- Comprehensive statistical techniques

- Strong community and support for data science applications

Java

Java is a general-purpose programming language that is known for its portability, scalability, and widespread use in enterprise environments. It is also used in AI development, particularly for large-scale machine learning.

- Libraries and Frameworks: Weka, Deeplearning4j, MOA, MLlib (for Apache Spark)

- Advantages:

- Portability across platforms

- Scalability for large-scale applications

- Strong integration with enterprise systems

- Robust performance

C++

C++ is a powerful low-level programming language that provides fine-grained control over system resources and performance. It is used in AI development where performance is critical, such as in gaming, real-time systems, and high-performance computing.

- Libraries and Frameworks: Dlib, Shark, DyNet, Caffe (secondary support)

- Advantages:

- High performance and efficiency

- Fine-grained control over system resources

- Suitable for real-time and high-performance applications

Julia

Julia is a high-level, high-performance programming language designed specifically for numerical and scientific computing. It is gaining traction in the AI community for its speed and ease of use in mathematical computation.

- Libraries and Frameworks: Flux.jl, Knet.jl, MLJ.jl, TextAnalysis.jl

- Advantages:

- High-performance execution

- Designed for numerical and scientific computing

- Easy integration with other programming languages

Popular AI Frameworks

AI frameworks provide essential tools and libraries that streamline the process of developing, training, and deploying machine learning models. Here's a look at some of the most popular frameworks:

TensorFlow

TensorFlow, developed by Google Brain, is one of the most widely used frameworks for deep learning. It provides a comprehensive ecosystem for building and deploying machine learning models at scale.

- Key Features:

- Support for multiple platforms, including mobile and edge devices

- TensorFlow Lite for mobile and embedded devices

- TensorFlow Serving for deploying models in production

- TensorFlow Extended (TFX) for end-to-end ML pipelines

PyTorch

PyTorch, developed by Facebook's AI Research lab, is another dominant framework in the deep learning community. It is known for its dynamic computation graph, which makes it intuitive and flexible for research and development.

- Key Features:

- Dynamic computation graph (eager execution)

- Strong support for GPU acceleration

- Extensive community and ecosystem

- Integration with native Python

scikit-learn

scikit-learn is a popular machine learning library in Python that provides simple and efficient tools for data mining, data analysis, and machine learning.

- Key Features:

- Easy-to-use API

- Comprehensive suite of classical ML algorithms

- Integration with NumPy, SciPy, and other scientific libraries

- Tools for model evaluation and validation

Keras

Keras is a high-level deep learning API written in Python, capable of running on top of TensorFlow, Microsoft Cognitive Toolkit (CNTK), or Theano. It provides a simple and fast interface for prototyping and building deep learning models.

- Key Features:

- User-friendly API

- Modular and extensible design

- Compatible with TensorFlow and other backends

- Support for both convolutional networks and recurrent networks

Apache Spark MLlib

Apache Spark MLlib is a scalable machine learning library built on top of Apache Spark. It provides tools for large-scale machine learning, data processing, and model training.

- Key Features:

- Scalable for big data applications

- Integration with Apache Spark for data processing

- Support for various machine learning algorithms

- Distributed training and evaluation

Caffe

Caffe is a deep learning framework developed by the Berkeley Vision and Learning Center (BVLC). It is known for its speed, modularity, and applicability to convolutional neural networks (CNNs).

- Key Features:

- High performance for image processing tasks

- Modular design for flexibility

- Extensive pre-trained model repository (Caffe Model Zoo)

- Focus on convolutional networks

Data Preparation and Preprocessing

Effective data preparation and preprocessing are crucial for developing accurate and robust AI models. This section covers the essential steps and techniques involved in preparing data for machine learning.

Data Collection

Data collection involves gathering relevant raw data from various sources. This can include structured data from databases, unstructured data from text and images, and time-series data from sensors. Key considerations for data collection include:

- Data Quality: Ensuring the data is accurate, complete, and relevant.

- Data Diversity: Gathering a diverse set of data samples to cover various scenarios.

- Ethical Considerations: Ensuring data collection adheres to ethical standards and privacy regulations.

Data Cleaning

Data cleaning involves correcting or removing incorrect, corrupted, or irrelevant data. It is a critical step to ensure the quality of the dataset and the effectiveness of the model.

- Handling Missing Values: Strategies include imputation (using mean, median, mode, or other statistical methods) or removing records with significant missing data.

- Outlier Detection: Identifying and handling outliers that could skew the results. This can be done using statistical methods or visualization techniques.

- Data Normalization/Standardization: Transforming data to a common scale without distorting differences in the ranges of values.

Feature Engineering

Feature engineering is the process of creating new features from raw data to improve the performance of machine learning models. It involves:

- Feature Extraction: Identifying key features from the data that are relevant to the problem.

- Feature Creation: Combining or transforming existing features to create new, more informative features.

- Dimensionality Reduction: Techniques like Principal Component Analysis (PCA) and t-Distributed Stochastic Neighbor Embedding (t-SNE) to reduce the number of features while preserving important information.

Data Transformation

Data transformation involves converting data into a suitable format for machine learning algorithms. This includes:

- Encoding Categorical Variables: Converting categorical data into numerical formats using techniques like one-hot encoding, label encoding, and binary encoding.

- Scaling: Adjusting the range of numerical features using techniques such as min-max scaling or z-score standardization.

- Text Processing: Converting text data into numerical representations using techniques like tokenization, stemming, lemmatization, and TF-IDF.

Data Splitting

Splitting the dataset into training, validation, and testing subsets is crucial for evaluating the performance of machine learning models.

- Training Set: The subset of data used to train the model.

- Validation Set: The subset of data used to fine-tune the model and select hyperparameters.

- Testing Set: The independent subset of data used to evaluate the final model's performance and generalization ability.

Data Augmentation

Data augmentation involves generating additional training samples from the existing data to improve the model's robustness and generalization.

- Image Augmentation: Techniques like rotation, scaling, translation, flipping, and adding noise to create new image samples.

- Text Augmentation: Techniques like synonym replacement, random insertion, and back-translation to create new text samples.

- Audio Augmentation: Techniques like time-shifting, pitch alteration, and adding background noise to create new audio samples.

Conclusion

The key technologies and tools discussed in this chapter play a critical role in advancing the field of AI. Programming languages like Python and R provide the foundation for developing AI applications, while frameworks such as TensorFlow, PyTorch, and scikit-learn offer powerful tools for creating and deploying models. Effective data preparation and preprocessing ensure that AI models are built on high-quality data, leading to better performance and reliability.

By understanding these foundational technologies and tools, you are well-equipped to embark on your AI journey, whether you are building cutting-edge applications or exploring the vast possibilities of artificial intelligence. The next chapters will delve deeper into practical applications, ethical considerations, and the future of AI, providing you with a comprehensive understanding of this transformative field.

Chapter 5: AI in Practice

Artificial Intelligence (AI) has moved from theory and research laboratories into real-world applications with significant impact across various industries. This chapter will explore the practical implementations of AI, delving into how it is transforming businesses, healthcare, autonomous systems, and more. By examining these diverse applications, we aim to illustrate the tangible benefits, challenges, and future potential of AI in everyday life.

Real-World Applications of AI

AI in Business and Industry

Enhancing Customer Experience

AI has revolutionized customer interactions through chatbots, virtual assistants, and personalized recommendation systems. These technologies improve efficiency and user satisfaction by providing immediate, relevant responses and suggestions.

- Chatbots and Virtual Assistants: AI-powered chatbots like those used by banks, e-commerce sites, and service-based companies can handle customer inquiries 24/7. Virtual assistants such as Siri, Alexa, and Google Assistant integrate seamlessly into users' daily routines, managing tasks from setting reminders to controlling smart home devices.

- Personalized Recommendations: E-commerce giants like Amazon and Netflix utilize AI algorithms to analyze user behavior and preferences, providing tailored product and content recommendations. This personalization boosts customer engagement and drives sales.

Operational Efficiency

AI-driven automation and optimization tools streamline business operations, leading to cost reductions and enhanced productivity.

- Supply Chain Management: AI algorithms optimize inventory management, predict demand, and streamline logistics. Companies like DHL and UPS use AI to maximize route efficiency and manage warehouse automation.

- Predictive Maintenance: In manufacturing, AI analyzes data from machinery to predict failures and schedule maintenance, reducing downtime. For example, General Electric uses AI-driven predictive models to maintain its equipment across various industries.

Enhanced Decision-Making

AI and machine learning provide insights by processing and analyzing large volumes of data, supporting better decision-making in real-time.

- Financial Analysis: Banks and investment firms use AI to detect fraudulent transactions, assess credit risk, and optimize trading strategies. AI algorithms analyze market data, news, and historical trends to make informed trading decisions.

- Human Resources: AI assists in recruitment by screening resumes, assessing candidates' suitability through video interview analysis, and predicting employee turnover. Companies like IBM leverage AI to enhance their HR processes, improving efficiency and reducing bias.

AI in Healthcare

AI is transforming healthcare by enhancing diagnostics, personalizing treatment, and improving patient outcomes. The integration of AI technologies has led to groundbreaking advancements and efficiencies in the medical field.

Diagnostics and Imaging

AI algorithms excel in analyzing medical imaging, offering quicker and often more accurate diagnoses than human radiologists.

- Radiology: AI-powered imaging analysis tools can detect anomalies in X-rays, MRIs, and CT scans with high precision. For instance, Google's DeepMind has developed AI models that can identify eye diseases from retinal scans and detect cancerous tissues in mammograms.

- Pathology: Machine learning models assist pathologists by analyzing tissue samples to identify cancerous cells and other abnormalities. This speeds up diagnosis and allows for early intervention.

Personalized Medicine

AI facilitates the customization of treatment plans based on individual patient data, leading to more effective therapies.

- Genomics: AI systems analyze vast amounts of genetic data to identify mutations and genetic profiles that can predict disease susceptibility and treatment response. Companies like 23andMe and Ancestry use AI-driven tools to offer insights into genetic predispositions and ancestry.

- Treatment Recommendations: By analyzing patient records, demographics, and clinical trials, AI systems like IBM Watson for Oncology can recommend personalized treatment plans, considering the most effective therapies based on individual patient factors.

Remote Monitoring and Telehealth

AI enhances telehealth by enabling remote patient monitoring, improving access to healthcare, and ensuring timely interventions.

- Wearable Health Devices: AI-powered wearables monitor vital signs such as heart rate, blood pressure, and glucose levels, alerting users and healthcare providers of potential health issues. Apple Watch and Fitbit devices use AI algorithms to detect irregular heart rhythms and other health metrics.

- Telemedicine Platforms: AI algorithms facilitate virtual consultations by analyzing patient data and providing diagnostic support to healthcare providers. Telemedicine platforms like Teladoc harness AI to triage patients and recommend appropriate care pathways.

AI in Autonomous Systems

AI is at the core of autonomous systems, ranging from self-driving cars to drones, transforming transportation, delivery, and various other industries.

Autonomous Vehicles

Self-driving cars represent one of the most prominent applications of AI, promising to revolutionize transportation by enhancing safety, reducing traffic congestion, and improving mobility.

- Perception and Navigation: AI algorithms process data from sensors like cameras, LIDAR, and radar to recognize and track objects, interpret road conditions, and navigate complex environments. Companies like Tesla, Waymo, and Uber employ sophisticated AI models enabling their vehicles to drive autonomously.

- Safety and Risk Management: AI-powered systems continuously monitor the vehicle's surroundings and make real-time decisions to avoid collisions and mitigate risks. Advanced driver-assistance systems (ADAS) such as lane-keeping assist, adaptive cruise control, and automatic emergency braking are interim steps towards full autonomy.

Drones and Robotics

AI-driven drones and robots are transforming industries by performing tasks that are hazardous, repetitive, or require precision.

- Agriculture: Drones equipped with AI plan and execute tasks like crop monitoring, pesticide application, and yield estimation. They analyze aerial imagery to assess crop health and detect issues such as pests or nutrient deficiencies. Companies like DJI and PrecisionHawk are leading the charge in agricultural drone technology.

- Logistics and Delivery: AI-powered drones and autonomous robots are streamlining logistics and delivery services. Companies like Amazon Prime Air and Zipline use drones for last-mile delivery and medical supply distribution in remote areas. Automated warehouse robots from companies like Kiva Systems (now part of Amazon Robotics) optimize storage and order fulfillment.

Industrial Automation

AI enhances industrial automation by integrating smart technologies into manufacturing processes, improving efficiency, and reducing human error.

- Robotic Process Automation (RPA): AI-driven RPA automates repetitive tasks such as data entry, document processing, and transaction processing, freeing human workers for higher-value tasks. Businesses adopt RPA to reduce operational costs and increase productivity.

- Quality Control: AI systems equipped with machine vision inspect products and components for defects with high accuracy and consistency. These systems are used in automotive, electronics, and consumer goods manufacturing to ensure quality standards.

Ethical Considerations and Challenges

While AI offers immense potential across various fields, it also presents ethical considerations and challenges that must be addressed to ensure responsible use and equitable benefits.

Bias and Fairness in AI

Sources of Bias

AI systems can inherit and amplify biases present in the data used to train them. This can lead to discriminatory outcomes in applications such as hiring, lending, and law enforcement.

- Historical Data: If the training data reflects historical biases or inequalities, the AI model may perpetuate these biases in its predictions and decisions. For example, biased criminal justice data can result in unfair sentencing recommendations.

- Algorithmic Bias: Biases can also stem from the design and implementation of the algorithms themselves. If an algorithm prioritizes certain features or overlooks others, it may produce skewed results.

Mitigating Bias

Addressing bias requires a multifaceted approach, including diverse data collection, transparent algorithm design, and ongoing evaluation.

- Diverse and Representative Data: Ensuring that training data is diverse and representative of different populations helps reduce bias. Continuous monitoring and updating of data can also improve fairness.

- Algorithmic Transparency: Clear documentation and transparency about how algorithms work and make decisions help identify and address biases. Explainable AI (XAI) techniques provide insights into the decision-making process of AI models.

- Fairness Audits: Regular fairness audits assess AI systems for biases and discriminatory outcomes. Organizations can use fairness metrics and bias-detection tools to evaluate and mitigate biases.

Privacy and Security Concerns

Data Privacy

AI systems often rely on large datasets, which can raise privacy concerns, especially when dealing with sensitive information such as health records, financial data, and personal identifiers.

- Data Anonymization: Techniques such as data anonymization and differential privacy protect individuals' identities while allowing data to be used for AI research and applications.

- Data Governance: Implementing robust data governance policies ensures that data is collected, stored, and used responsibly. Organizations must comply with data protection regulations like GDPR and CCPA.

Security Risks

AI systems can be vulnerable to attacks that compromise their integrity, accuracy, and confidentiality.

- Adversarial Attacks: Attackers can manipulate input data to deceive AI models, leading to incorrect predictions or classifications. For example, adding subtle perturbations to an image can cause a computer vision system to misidentify the object.

- Model Theft: AI models themselves can be stolen or reverse-engineered, revealing proprietary information and potentially compromising security. Protecting AI models with techniques like model watermarking and encryption helps mitigate this risk.

Accountability and Responsibility

As AI systems take on more decision-making roles, determining accountability and responsibility becomes crucial.

- Human-in-the-Loop: Ensuring human oversight in critical AI applications, such as medical diagnoses and autonomous vehicles, helps maintain accountability. Humans can intervene and review AI decisions, providing an additional layer of responsibility.

- Ethical Guidelines and Standards: Developing ethical guidelines and industry standards for AI use promotes responsible development and deployment. Initiatives like the AI Ethics Guidelines from organizations like the IEEE and the European Commission provide frameworks for ethical AI practices.

Future of AI in Practice

The future of AI holds exciting possibilities and challenges as the technology continues to evolve.

Emerging Trends

- Edge AI: AI processing at the edge, closer to data sources such as IoT devices and sensors, reduces latency and enhances real-time decision-making. Edge AI enables faster and more efficient applications in fields like autonomous vehicles, smart cities, and industrial automation.

- Federated Learning: Federated learning enables collaborative model training across decentralized devices while preserving data privacy. This approach is particularly useful in healthcare and finance, where data privacy is paramount.

- Explainable AI: Enhancing transparency and interpretability of AI models through explainable AI techniques builds trust and facilitates adoption, particularly in regulated industries.

Predictions and Speculations

- AI-Powered Healthcare: AI will continue to revolutionize healthcare with advancements in diagnostics, personalized medicine, and remote patient care. Predictive analytics will enable early disease detection and preventive interventions.

- AI in Education: AI-powered personalized learning platforms will enhance education by adapting to individual student needs, providing real-time feedback, and facilitating remote learning.

- AI and the Future of Work: AI will transform the workforce, automating routine tasks and augmenting human capabilities. Reskilling and upskilling programs will be essential to prepare the workforce for AI-driven job roles.

The Role of AI in Society

AI has the potential to address some of society's most pressing challenges, from climate change to social justice. However, realizing this potential requires a collaborative approach involving governments, organizations, researchers, and the public.

- Climate Action: AI can contribute to climate action by optimizing energy consumption, enhancing renewable energy sources, and predicting environmental changes. AI models can monitor and mitigate the impacts of climate change on ecosystems and communities.

- Social Good: AI applications in areas like disaster response, healthcare access, and poverty alleviation can promote social good and improve the quality of life for marginalized populations. Collaborative initiatives like AI for Good harness AI for humanitarian and social causes.

Conclusion

The practical applications of AI are vast and transformative, touching every aspect of our lives. From enhancing business operations and revolutionizing healthcare to driving autonomous systems and addressing ethical considerations, AI is reshaping the world in profound ways. As we continue to harness the power of AI, it is crucial to navigate the challenges and ethical implications responsibly, ensuring that AI benefits all of humanity.

In the following chapters, we will delve deeper into other critical aspects of AI, including core techniques, key technologies, and the future landscape of this dynamic field. With "Artificial Intelligence: Only the Essentials," we aim to provide you with the knowledge and insights to understand and engage with AI in meaningful ways, enriching your learning journey and sparking thoughtful conversations about the future of AI.

Chapter 6: Ethical Considerations and Challenges

Introduction

As Artificial Intelligence (AI) continues to permeate various facets of society, the ethical considerations and challenges associated with its development and deployment become increasingly vital to address. This chapter delves into the multifaceted ethical paradigms and practical concerns surrounding AI, examining issues such as bias and fairness, privacy and security, accountability, and the broader societal impacts. The goal is to equip you with a comprehensive understanding of the ethical landscape, fostering critical thought and responsible discussions about the future of AI.

Bias and Fairness in AI

AI systems are not intrinsically objective; they are products of the data they are trained on and the humans who develop them. This can lead to bias and fairness issues that can have significant real-world consequences.

Sources of Bias

1. Data Bias: The training data used to develop AI models can contain biases that reflect historical prejudices or socio-economic inequalities. If an AI system is trained on biased data, it can perpetuate and even amplify these biases.

- Example: In recruitment algorithms, if historical data shows a preference for male candidates over female candidates, the AI might favor male applicants, thereby reinforcing gender biases.

2. Algorithmic Bias: The design and implementation of algorithms can introduce biases. For example, certain features or decision rules may disproportionately affect specific groups.

- Example: Facial recognition systems have been shown to have higher error rates for people with darker skin tones, reflecting biases in the training datasets and the algorithmic processes used.

3. Interaction Bias: Users' interactions with AI systems can introduce new biases. For instance, if a chatbot learns from user interactions, it might pick up on and replicate harmful language or stereotypes.

Mitigating Bias and Ensuring Fairness

1. Diverse Data Collection: Ensuring that training data is representative of all relevant demographics and scenarios can help mitigate bias.

- Strategy: Actively seek out and include diverse data sources, and continually update datasets to reflect changing conditions and populations.

2. Bias Detection and Correction Tools: Using tools and techniques to identify and correct biases in datasets and algorithms is crucial.

- Example: Techniques like re-sampling, re-weighting, and adversarial debiasing can help address bias in machine learning models.

3. Transparency and Explainability: Transparent and interpretable AI systems allow stakeholders to understand how decisions are made, facilitating the identification and correction of biases.

- Strategy: Develop algorithms that provide clear insights into their decision-making processes, and create user interfaces that explain AI behavior in understandable terms.

4. Inclusive Teams: Diverse development teams can bring various perspectives and help identify potential biases that others might overlook.

- Action: Encourage diversity in AI research and development teams, including a mix of genders, ethnicities, disciplines, and backgrounds.

Privacy and Security Concerns

AI systems often require vast amounts of data, some of which can be sensitive and personal. This raises critical privacy and security issues that need to be carefully managed.

Data Privacy

1. Data Collection and Consent: Obtaining informed consent from individuals whose data is being collected is a fundamental privacy principle. However, in practice, users often do not fully understand or have control over how their data is used.

- Best Practice: Implement clear and concise consent forms, regularly update users about how their data is used, and provide easy-to-use options for users to withdraw consent.

2. Data Anonymization: Anonymizing data can protect individual privacy, but it is not foolproof. Techniques such as de-anonymization can re-identify individuals in supposedly anonymous datasets.

- Example: Netflix's anonymized movie ratings dataset was de-anonymized by correlating it with user data from IMDb, revealing individuals' identities.

3. Data Minimization: Collecting and retaining only the data necessary for a specific purpose can reduce privacy risks.

- Strategy: Adhere to the principle of data minimization, and employ edge computing where data processing occurs locally on the device, reducing the need to transfer sensitive information to centralized servers.

Security Issues

1. Data Breaches: AI systems are attractive targets for cyberattacks due to the valuable data they hold. Data breaches can lead to significant harm, including identity theft and financial loss.

- Best Practice: Employ robust cybersecurity measures, such as encryption, firewalls, intrusion detection systems, and regular security audits.

2. Adversarial Attacks: AI models can be vulnerable to adversarial attacks, where malicious actors manipulate input data to deceive the system.

- Example: In image recognition, adding subtle, imperceptible noise to an image can cause the AI to misclassify it.

- Mitigation: Develop and deploy adversarial training techniques, robustness testing, and anomaly detection systems to defend against such attacks.

3. System Integrity: Ensuring the integrity of AI systems is crucial, as compromised systems can lead to erroneous decisions and actions.

- Strategy: Implement measures such as secure software development practices, regular integrity checks, and continuous monitoring of AI systems.

Accountability and Responsibility

AI systems can make decisions with significant ethical and legal implications, raising complex questions about accountability and responsibility.

Who is Responsible?

1. Developers and Engineers: Those who design and implement AI systems bear responsibility for ensuring their ethical use and addressing potential harms.

- Ethical Duty: Follow ethical guidelines and industry standards, such as the IEEE Global Initiative on Ethics of Autonomous and Intelligent Systems.

2. Organizations: Companies and institutions deploying AI must be accountable for their systems' impacts, including ensuring compliance with laws and regulations.

- Corporate Responsibility: Adopt AI ethics frameworks, conduct impact assessments, and establish oversight committees to monitor AI use.

3. Regulators and Policymakers: Governments and regulatory bodies have a role in creating and enforcing laws and guidelines to ensure the responsible development and use of AI.

- Policy Actions: Develop and implement comprehensive regulations that address data protection, algorithmic transparency, and accountability mechanisms.

Legal and Ethical Frameworks

1. Regulatory Landscape: Different countries and regions are developing AI regulations, such as the European Union's proposed AI Act, which aims to regulate AI systems based on their risk levels.

- Stay Informed: Keep abreast of international regulatory trends, and align AI practices with relevant legal requirements.

2. Ethical AI Principles: Universal principles, such as those proposed by organizations like the Partnership on AI, include fairness, transparency, privacy, accountability, and safety.

- Implementation: Translate these high-level principles into actionable guidelines and best practices within your organization.

Ensuring Accountability

1. Auditability: AI systems should be auditable, allowing for independent evaluation to ensure compliance with ethical standards and regulations.

- Strategy: Employ third-party audits, maintain detailed documentation, and implement change management processes.

2. Redress Mechanisms: Establishing mechanisms for users to challenge and seek redress for decisions made by AI systems is crucial for accountability.

- Action Steps: Create clear channels for complaints, provide human oversight for AI decisions, and ensure timely resolution of issues.

Societal Impacts

The deployment of AI has broad societal impacts, influencing areas such as employment, inequality, and democratic processes.

Impact on Employment

1. Job Displacement vs. Job Creation: AI can automate certain tasks, leading to job displacement, but it can also create new opportunities and industries.

- Adaptive Strategies: Support workforce retraining and education programs, encourage lifelong learning, and promote the development of skills for the AI-driven economy.

2. Changing Nature of Work: The integration of AI into the workplace can change job roles, requiring a shift in how tasks are performed and managed.

- Proactive Measures: Foster a culture of adaptability, redefine job descriptions, and empower employees to work alongside AI tools effectively.

Inequality and Access

1. Digital Divide: The benefits of AI are not evenly distributed, and access to AI technologies can exacerbate existing inequalities.

- Initiatives: Support policies and programs that promote digital inclusion and provide access to AI education and resources for underserved communities.

2. Economic Inequality: AI-driven economic growth can lead to increased wealth concentration if not managed equitably.

- Policy Interventions: Explore mechanisms such as progressive taxation, universal basic income, and social safety nets to address potential economic disparities.

Impact on Democracy

1. Misinformation and Manipulation: AI can be used to spread misinformation and manipulate public opinion, posing threats to democratic processes.

- Countermeasures: Develop and deploy AI tools to detect and counter misinformation, promote media literacy, and encourage responsible AI use in political campaigns.

2. Surveillance and Civil Liberties: AI-powered surveillance systems can infringe on privacy and civil liberties if not properly regulated.

- Regulatory Balance: Implement safeguards that protect privacy rights while ensuring public safety and security. Promote transparency and accountability in surveillance practices.

Conclusion

The ethical considerations and challenges of AI are complex and multifaceted, encompassing issues of bias, fairness, privacy, security, accountability, and broader societal impacts. Addressing these concerns requires a collaborative effort from developers, organizations, regulators, and society at large. By fostering a culture of ethical awareness and responsibility, we can harness the power of AI to benefit humanity while mitigating potential harms.

In this chapter, we have explored the critical ethical dimensions of AI, providing insights and strategies to navigate these challenges. As AI continues to evolve, ongoing engagement with ethical principles and thoughtful reflection on the implications of AI technologies will be essential to ensuring a just and equitable future.

The following chapters will delve into the future of AI, practical guidance for getting started with AI, and enlightening case studies, further enriching your understanding of this transformative field. Stay informed, stay ethical, and continue your journey with AI knowledge.

Chapter 7: The Future of AI

Emerging Trends

As we journey through the 21st century, artificial intelligence (AI) continues to evolve at an unprecedented pace, driven by ever-increasing computational power, vast datasets, and advanced algorithms. Emerging trends in AI research and development promise to not only transform existing industries but also create entirely new avenues of innovation and possibility. In this chapter, we will explore some of the most promising and transformative trends that are shaping the future of AI.

Explainable AI (XAI)

One of the challenges in current AI systems, especially those based on deep learning, is the lack of transparency in their decision-making processes. This "black box" nature can be problematic, particularly in critical applications such as healthcare, finance, and criminal justice, where understanding the rationale behind AI decisions is essential.

Explainable AI (XAI) seeks to address this issue by developing methods and tools that make AI systems more interpretable and understandable to humans. By offering insights into how an AI model arrives at its conclusions, XAI can help build trust, ensure accountability, and facilitate the adoption of AI in high-stakes domains.

- Techniques in XAI:

- Model-Agnostic Approaches: Tools like LIME (Local Interpretable Model-agnostic Explanations) and SHAP (SHapley Additive exPlanations) provide explanations for any machine learning model by approximating its behavior locally.

- Interpretable Models: Designing models that are inherently interpretable, such as decision trees, rule-based systems, and linear models.

- Visualization Methods: Visual tools that help users understand the inner workings of complex AI models, such as feature importance plots, saliency maps, and activation maximization.

Federated Learning

The traditional approach of training AI models often involves centralizing vast amounts of data in a single location, which can raise concerns about privacy, security, and data ownership. Federated learning offers an alternative paradigm by enabling AI models to be trained collaboratively across multiple decentralized devices or servers while keeping the data where it is generated.

- How It Works:

- Local Training: AI models are trained locally on devices (such as smartphones or edge devices) using local data.

- Model Updates: The local models' updates (not the data itself) are sent to a central server, which aggregates them to improve the global model.

- Repeat Process: The updated global model is then sent back to the devices, and the cycle continues.

Federated learning holds great promise for applications where data privacy is paramount, such as healthcare, finance, and IoT (Internet of Things) environments.

Autonomous Systems

Autonomous systems, which include self-driving cars, drones, and robotic assistants, are rapidly advancing and hold the potential to revolutionize various industries. These systems rely on AI to perceive their environment, make decisions, and perform actions, often in real-time and without human intervention.

- Key Components:

- Perception: Using sensors such as cameras, LiDAR, and radar to gather information about the environment.

- Decision-Making: Applying algorithms to process sensor data and make informed decisions on actions to take.

- Actuation: Executing actions through motors, actuators, or other mechanisms.

AI in Edge Computing

Edge computing refers to processing data closer to where it is generated, rather than relying on centralized cloud servers. AI in edge computing enables real-time decision-making with reduced latency, improved privacy, and reduced bandwidth usage.

- Applications:

- Industrial IoT: Real-time monitoring and predictive maintenance in manufacturing plants.

- Smart Cities: Traffic management, surveillance, and public safety.

- Healthcare: Remote patient monitoring and diagnosis.

Ethical AI and Responsible AI

As AI systems become more integrated into society, ethical considerations and responsible deployment have become critical. Ethical AI and responsible AI initiatives focus on ensuring that AI technologies are developed and used in ways that are fair, transparent, and aligned with human values.

- Key Principles:

- Fairness and Bias Mitigation: Ensuring that AI systems do not perpetuate or amplify biases present in training data.

- Transparency and Accountability: Providing clear documentation and explanations for AI decisions.

- Privacy: Protecting individuals' data and ensuring consent.

- Inclusivity: Designing AI systems that are accessible and beneficial to all demographic groups.

AI and Quantum Computing

Quantum computing has the potential to revolutionize AI by providing unprecedented computational power. While still in its early stages, quantum computing could solve complex problems that are currently intractable for classical computers.

- Potential Synergies:

- Optimization Problems: Quantum algorithms could dramatically improve optimization tasks, such as supply chain logistics and financial modeling.

- Machine Learning: Quantum machine learning algorithms could accelerate the training of AI models and tackle problems intractable by classical methods.

Predictions and Speculations

While predicting the future is inherently uncertain, examining current trends and historical patterns offers valuable insights into where AI might be headed.

Short-Term (1-5 Years)

- Continued Deployment of Narrow AI: Narrow AI systems will become even more pervasive in everyday applications, from virtual assistants and chatbots to recommendation systems and personalized services.

- Improved Human-AI Collaboration: Enhanced tools and interfaces will enable more effective collaboration between humans and AI, with AI augmenting human skills and decision-making.

- Advancements in Healthcare AI: AI will become more integrated into healthcare, from diagnostics and treatment recommendations to personalized medicine and drug discovery.

Medium-Term (5-15 Years)

- Breakthroughs in AGI Research: Researchers may make significant strides towards Artificial General Intelligence (AGI), although achieving true AGI remains uncertain and highly challenging.

- Transformation of Transportation: Autonomous vehicles may become commonplace, fundamentally changing transportation systems, reducing accidents, and improving mobility.

- AI-Driven Scientific Discovery: AI will play a critical role in accelerating scientific research, from discovering new materials and drugs to advancing our understanding of complex systems.

Long-Term (15+ Years)

- Potential Emergence of ASI: If research progresses, the emergence of Artificial Superintelligence (ASI) could become a reality, with profound and far-reaching implications for humanity.

- Ubiquitous AI Integration: AI may become seamlessly integrated into every aspect of daily life, from smart homes and cities to personalized learning and entertainment experiences.

- Ethical and Societal Considerations: As AI becomes more pervasive, ethical considerations, regulations, and societal impacts will be of paramount importance. Ensuring that AI benefits all of humanity will be a critical challenge.

The Role of AI in Society

Economic Impacts

AI is poised to have significant economic impacts across various sectors. Automation, driven by AI, can lead to increased efficiency and productivity, but it also raises concerns about job displacement and workforce transitions.

- Productivity Gains: AI can automate repetitive tasks, optimize supply chains, and enhance decision-making, leading to increased productivity and economic growth.

- Job Displacement and Creation: While some jobs may be displaced by automation, AI is also expected to create new opportunities in fields such as AI research, data science, and AI ethics. Reskilling and upskilling the workforce will be essential to navigate these changes.

- Economic Inequality: The unequal distribution of AI benefits could exacerbate economic inequality. Policies and initiatives to ensure equitable access to AI technologies and their benefits will be crucial.

Social and Cultural Impacts

AI has the potential to reshape societal norms, cultural practices, and human interactions. Understanding and addressing these impacts will be critical for fostering a society where AI enhances human well-being.

- Human-AI Interaction: As AI systems become more integrated into daily life, the nature of human-AI interaction will evolve. Ensuring that these interactions are positive, respectful, and aligned with human values will be important.

- Cultural Representation in AI: AI systems trained on diverse and representative data can help preserve and promote cultural heritage, language, and identity. Efforts to ensure cultural inclusivity in AI will be vital.

- Ethical and Moral Implications: The use of AI in areas such as social scoring, surveillance, and autonomous weapons raises profound ethical and moral questions. Societal dialogue and ethical frameworks will be necessary to navigate these complex issues.

Environmental Impacts

AI can play a crucial role in addressing global challenges such as climate change, resource management, and environmental sustainability.

- Climate Change Mitigation: AI can enhance climate modeling, optimize energy consumption, and support the development of renewable energy sources.

- Sustainable Resource Management: AI can be used to monitor and manage natural resources, reduce waste, and promote sustainable agricultural practices.

- Environmental Monitoring: AI-powered sensors and analytics can track environmental changes, detect pollution, and support conservation efforts.

Ethical and Legal Implications

The ethical and legal implications of AI are of paramount importance as the technology becomes more pervasive. Establishing robust ethical guidelines, regulatory frameworks, and governance structures will be essential.

- AI Ethics: Developing principles and guidelines to ensure that AI systems are fair, transparent, and aligned with human values.

- Regulation and Governance: Creating regulatory frameworks to oversee the development and deployment of AI, balancing innovation with societal protections.

- Global Cooperation: International collaboration and cooperation will be necessary to address the global nature of AI's challenges and opportunities.

Conclusion

The future of AI holds immense promise and potential, but it also presents significant challenges and uncertainties. As we forge ahead, it is imperative to approach AI development and deployment with a sense of responsibility, foresight, and ethical consideration.

In this chapter, we have explored the emerging trends, predictions, and the broader role of AI in society. By staying informed, engaging in thoughtful dialogue, and fostering collaborative efforts, we can navigate the complexities of AI's future and harness its transformative power for the benefit of all humanity.

As we continue to explore the depths of artificial intelligence, let us remain guided by the principles of fairness, transparency, and human-centered values. The journey is far from over, and the story of AI is still being written. Together, we can shape a future where AI acts as a force for good, enhancing our lives and advancing our collective potential.

Chapter 8: Getting Started with AI

Artificial Intelligence (AI) has rapidly evolved from a niche academic discipline to a pivotal technology that permeates various facets of modern life. The desire to navigate and master this expansive field can be both exciting and daunting. This chapter aims to demystify the entry points into the world of AI, offering a comprehensive guide to learning resources, practical steps for building your first AI model, and potential career pathways. Whether you are a novice or have some experience, this chapter will equip you with the foundational knowledge and strategies to embark on your AI journey.

Learning Resources

The first step in getting started with AI is filling your arsenal with the proper resources. With abundance comes the challenge of choosing quality materials. Here, we break down various types of resources: books, online courses, tutorials, forums, and hands-on projects.

Books

Books can provide in-depth knowledge and are excellent for understanding the theoretical underpinnings of AI. Here are some highly recommended reads:

- "Artificial Intelligence: A Modern Approach" by Stuart Russell and Peter Norvig: Often considered the AI bible, this comprehensive text covers a broad spectrum of AI topics, from the basics to advanced machine learning techniques.

- "Deep Learning" by Ian Goodfellow, Yoshua Bengio, and Aaron Courville: This book offers a deep dive into neural networks and deep learning, making it ideal for readers with some background in mathematics and programming.

- "Machine Learning Yearning" by Andrew Ng: This is a practical guide that provides insights into the machine learning process, written by one of the leading figures in the field.

Online Courses

Online courses allow for interactive learning and often come with forums for community support. Here are some notable platforms and courses:

- Coursera:

- "Machine Learning" by Andrew Ng: A highly acclaimed course offering a broad overview of machine learning concepts and algorithms.

- "Deep Learning Specialization" by Andrew Ng: This series of courses covers everything from neural networks to convolutional networks, sequence models, and more.

- edX:

- "MicroMasters Program in Artificial Intelligence by Columbia University": Offers a series of rigorous graduate-level courses in AI, providing a deep understanding of the subject.

- Udacity:

- "AI Programming with Python Nanodegree": Focuses on the technical skills needed for AI development, including Python, NumPy, and TensorFlow.

Tutorials and Blogs

Tutorials and blogs can be great for hands-on learning and keeping up with the latest advancements in AI. Here are some useful resources:

- Kaggle: Offers a plethora of datasets and tutorials to practice machine learning problems.

- Towards Data Science: A Medium publication that hosts articles and tutorials from the AI community.

- Fast.ai: Provides practical deep learning courses and tutorials that emphasize ethical AI practices.

Forums and Community Support

The AI community is vibrant and collaborative. Engaging with forums can lead to valuable insights and troubleshooting help:

- Stack Overflow: A go-to platform for programming-related questions, including AI and machine learning.

- Reddit: Subreddits like r/MachineLearning, r/deeplearning, and r/artificial offer discussions, news, and advice.

- GitHub: Many open-source AI projects and repositories. Reviewing other people's code and contributing to projects can be excellent learning experiences.

Hands-On Projects

Learning by doing is invaluable in AI. Here are some suggestions for beginner-friendly projects:

- Image Classification with CNNs: Build a convolutional neural network (CNN) to classify images (e.g., cats vs. dogs).

- Sentiment Analysis with NLP: Use natural language processing (NLP) techniques to analyze the sentiment of social media posts or product reviews.

- Recommendation Systems: Create a system that recommends movies or books based on user preferences.

- Self-Driving Car Simulation: Use reinforcement learning to create a simple self-driving car in a simulated environment.

Building Your First AI Model

Once you've accumulated knowledge from various sources, it's time to get your hands dirty. Building your first AI model is a significant milestone and can be highly rewarding. Here's a step-by-step guide to walk you through the process:

Step 1: Define the Problem

The first step in any AI project is clearly defining the problem you're trying to solve. This could be anything from predicting house prices to classifying emails as spam or non-spam. For this guide, let's consider a simple problem: predicting house prices based on features like size, number of rooms, and location.

Step 2: Data Collection and Cleaning

The quality of your data significantly affects the performance of your AI model. Here's how to go about it:

- Data Collection: Gather a dataset that includes features and labels. For example, a dataset of houses with details like size, number of rooms, location, and their selling prices. You can often find free datasets on sites like Kaggle or UCI Machine Learning Repository.

- Data Cleaning: Clean your data to ensure it's free of errors and inconsistencies. This includes dealing with missing values, removing duplicates, and correcting any inaccuracies. Tools like pandas in Python are immensely useful for this purpose.

Step 3: Exploratory Data Analysis (EDA)

Conducting EDA helps in understanding the relationships between variables and identifying any patterns or anomalies. This involves:

- Visualizing Data: Use charts and graphs to get a visual sense of the data. Libraries like Matplotlib and Seaborn in Python can be useful.

- Statistical Analysis: Calculate summary statistics like mean, median, and standard deviation. Look at correlations between variables to gain insights.

Step 4: Feature Engineering

Feature engineering involves selecting, modifying, or creating new features to improve the performance of your model:

- Normalization: Scale your features so they fit within a specific range, typically 0 to 1. This helps in speeding up the learning process.

- Categorical Encoding: Convert categorical variables into numerical values. Techniques like one-hot encoding can be used.

Step 5: Model Selection

Choose an appropriate model for your problem. For our house price prediction example, you might start with a simple linear regression model:

- Linear Regression: This statistical method models the relationship between the dependent variable (house price) and one or more independent variables (size, number of rooms, location, etc.).

Step 6: Model Training

Split your data into training and testing sets, typically 80-20 or 70-30:

- Training the Model: Fit your model to the training data using libraries like Scikit-learn in Python.

- Hyperparameter Tuning: Experiment with different hyperparameters to optimize your model's performance.

Step 7: Model Evaluation

Evaluate the performance of your model on the test set:

- Metrics: Use metrics like Mean Squared Error (MSE) or R-squared to evaluate performance.

- Cross-Validation: Use k-fold cross-validation to ensure that your model generalizes well to unseen data.

Step 8: Model Deployment

Once satisfied with the model's performance, you can deploy it in a production environment. Tools like Flask or Django can help you create a web API for your model, making it accessible to other applications.

Career Pathways in AI

As the adoption of AI continues to grow, so do the career opportunities. Here are some of the potential career pathways:

Data Scientist

Data scientists analyze and interpret complex data to help organizations make better decisions. They employ statistical methods, machine learning, and data visualization techniques to extract actionable insights.

Skills Required:

- Proficiency in programming languages like Python or R.

- Strong understanding of statistics and probability.

- Knowledge of machine learning algorithms and techniques.

- Expertise in data manipulation and visualization tools.

Machine Learning Engineer

Machine learning engineers are responsible for designing, training, and deploying machine learning models. They work closely with data scientists and software engineers to integrate models into products.

Skills Required:

- Advanced knowledge of machine learning algorithms and frameworks (e.g., TensorFlow, PyTorch).

- Proficiency in software development practices.

- Experience with cloud platforms (AWS, Google Cloud, Azure).

- Strong math and statistics background.

AI Research Scientist

AI research scientists focus on advancing the field by developing new algorithms, improving existing methodologies, and publishing their findings.

Skills Required:

- Deep understanding of machine learning and AI fundamentals.

- Strong programming and analytical skills.

- Background in mathematics, particularly linear algebra, calculus, and probability.

- Experience with research methodologies and academic writing.

AI Product Manager

AI product managers oversee the development and deployment of AI-driven products. They act as a liaison between tech teams, business stakeholders, and customers to ensure successful product outcomes.

Skills Required:

- Understanding of AI and machine learning fundamentals.

- Strong project management and leadership skills.

- Ability to communicate complex technical concepts to non-technical stakeholders.

- Experience with product lifecycle management.

AI Ethicist

AI ethicists ensure that AI systems are designed and deployed in a manner that is ethical and fair. They address issues related to bias, privacy, accountability, and transparency.

Skills Required:

- Deep understanding of ethical principles and their application to AI.

- Experience with policy development and regulatory compliance.

- Strong communication and advocacy skills.

- Background in philosophy, law, or related fields.

AI Consultant

AI consultants help organizations identify opportunities to leverage AI, develop strategies, and implement AI solutions. They work across various industries, providing expert advice and tailored solutions.

Skills Required:

- Broad understanding of AI applications across different industries.

- Strong analytical and problem-solving skills.

- Excellent communication and presentation abilities.

- Experience with project management and consulting practices.

Conclusion

Getting started with AI is a journey that combines theoretical learning with practical application. With the right resources, dedication, and curiosity, you can navigate the complex world of AI and carve out a fulfilling and impactful career. The field is ever-evolving, offering opportunities for continuous learning and discovery. As you proceed, remember that the key to mastery lies in persistent effort, collaboration, and a passion for innovation.

Whether you are aiming to become a data scientist, machine learning engineer, AI researcher, or any other AI professional, the foundational steps outlined in this chapter will set you on the right path. Embrace the challenges, celebrate the breakthroughs, and contribute to the vibrant and transformative field of artificial intelligence.

Chapter 9: Case Studies

Studying real-world applications of artificial intelligence (AI) provides valuable insights into its practical implementations, successes, and challenges. This chapter presents various case studies that illustrate how AI has transformed industries, solved complex problems, and paved the way for future innovations. Each case study includes an overview of the problem, the AI approach taken, the results achieved, and lessons learned.

Case Study 1: Healthcare - Diagnosing Diabetic Retinopathy

Overview of the Problem

Diabetic retinopathy is a complication of diabetes that affects the eyes and can lead to blindness if not detected and treated early. Manual screening for the disease is resource-intensive and requires trained ophthalmologists, which limits access to timely diagnosis, especially in under-resourced areas.

AI Approach

To address this issue, researchers developed a deep learning-based system using convolutional neural networks (CNNs) to automatically analyze retinal images for signs of diabetic retinopathy. The AI model was trained on a large dataset of retinal images labeled by expert ophthalmologists.

Results Achieved

The AI system demonstrated high accuracy in detecting diabetic retinopathy, on par with, and in some cases exceeding, the performance of human specialists. It was able to identify the signs of the disease in seconds, significantly speeding up the diagnostic process and enabling large-scale screening programs in regions lacking ophthalmologists.

70

Lessons Learned

- Data Quality is Crucial: High-quality, well-labeled data was essential for training the AI model effectively.

- Access to Care: AI can play a pivotal role in improving access to healthcare in underserved communities.

- Collaboration: Successful implementation required collaboration between AI researchers, medical professionals, and policymakers.

Case Study 2: Automotive Industry - Autonomous Vehicles

Overview of the Problem

Developing fully autonomous vehicles (self-driving cars) has the potential to revolutionize transportation by reducing accidents, decreasing traffic congestion, and improving mobility for individuals unable to drive.

AI Approach

Companies like Waymo, Tesla, and Uber have leveraged a combination of AI techniques, including computer vision, machine learning, and sensor fusion, to develop self-driving systems. These systems use data from cameras, lidar, radar, and ultrasonic sensors to perceive the environment and make driving decisions.

Results Achieved

Autonomous vehicles have made significant progress, with certain models achieving high levels of autonomy in controlled environments. Waymo's autonomous taxis, for instance, have successfully transported passengers in selected cities without a human driver.

Lessons Learned

- Safety is Paramount: Ensuring the safety and reliability of autonomous vehicles requires extensive testing and validation.

- Ethical and Legal Considerations: The deployment of self-driving cars raises important questions about liability, insurance, and regulatory frameworks.

- Human-AI Interaction: Understanding how humans and autonomous systems interact is crucial for the smooth integration of self-driving technologies.

Case Study 3: Financial Services - Fraud Detection

Overview of the Problem

Fraudulent activities in financial transactions pose significant risks to banks and their customers, leading to financial losses and damaged reputations. Traditional rule-based systems for fraud detection are often insufficient due to the evolving nature of fraudulent schemes.

AI Approach

Financial institutions have adopted machine learning models to enhance fraud detection capabilities. These models analyze vast amounts of transaction data, identifying patterns and anomalies that signal potential fraud. Techniques such as supervised learning, unsupervised learning, and anomaly detection are commonly used.

Results Achieved

AI-powered fraud detection systems have dramatically improved the accuracy and speed of identifying fraudulent transactions. For example, PayPal uses machine learning algorithms to analyze millions of transactions per day, reducing false positives and detecting fraud with high precision.

Lessons Learned

- Continuous Learning: Fraudsters constantly adapt their tactics, so fraud detection systems must be regularly updated and retrained.

- Data Privacy: Balancing the need for data to train AI models with the privacy concerns of customers is critical.

- Integration and Usability: Successful deployment requires integrating AI systems with existing financial infrastructure and ensuring they are user-friendly for analysts.

Case Study 4: Retail - Personalized Recommendations

Overview of the Problem

Providing personalized product recommendations to customers can significantly boost sales and enhance the shopping experience. Traditional recommendation systems often struggle with scale and accuracy.

AI Approach

Retailers like Amazon and Netflix use machine learning algorithms to create personalized recommendation engines. Techniques such as collaborative filtering, content-based filtering, and deep learning are employed to analyze user behavior and preferences.

Results Achieved

Personalized recommendation systems have proven highly effective, driving a substantial portion of sales and customer engagement. For example, Amazon's recommendation engine accounts for a significant percentage of its revenue, showcasing the power of targeted suggestions.

Lessons Learned

- Data is the Foundation: Access to diverse and large datasets is essential for training accurate recommendation models.

- User Experience Matters: Recommendations must be relevant and timely, enhancing rather than disrupting the user experience.

- Scalability: Systems must be designed to handle large-scale data processing and deliver real-time recommendations.

Case Study 5: Agriculture - Precision Farming

Overview of the Problem

Farmers face challenges such as optimizing crop yields, reducing resource usage, and managing pests and diseases. Traditional farming methods often lack the precision needed to address these issues efficiently.

AI Approach

AI techniques, including computer vision, machine learning, and remote sensing, are used in precision farming to monitor crop health, soil conditions, and weather patterns. Drones and satellite imagery provide data that AI models analyze to offer actionable insights.

Results Achieved

Precision farming has led to significant improvements in crop management, resource optimization, and yield forecasting. AI-driven systems help farmers make data-informed decisions, reducing costs and enhancing sustainability.

Lessons Learned

- Integration with Traditional Practices: Combining AI with farmers' expertise and traditional practices enhances overall effectiveness.

- Environmental Impact: Precision farming contributes to sustainable agriculture by optimizing resource use and minimizing waste.

- Accessibility: Ensuring AI tools are accessible and user-friendly for farmers, particularly in developing regions, is crucial for broad adoption.

Case Study 6: Manufacturing - Predictive Maintenance

Overview of the Problem

Unexpected equipment failures in manufacturing can lead to costly downtime and production delays. Traditional maintenance schedules often result in either over-maintenance or under-maintenance.

AI Approach

Predictive maintenance uses AI and machine learning models to analyze data from sensors embedded in machinery. These models predict equipment failures before they occur, allowing for timely maintenance and preventing unplanned downtime.

Results Achieved

Predictive maintenance systems have significantly reduced downtime and maintenance costs, improving overall operational efficiency. Companies like General Electric and Siemens have successfully implemented AI-driven predictive maintenance in their manufacturing processes.

Lessons Learned

- Data Collection: High-quality sensor data is essential for accurate predictions.

- Cost-Benefit Analysis: Implementing predictive maintenance requires an initial investment, balanced by long-term savings.

- Cultural Shift: Adoption often necessitates a cultural shift within organizations, emphasizing proactive rather than reactive maintenance practices.

Case Study 7: Entertainment - Content Generation

Overview of the Problem

The entertainment industry faces high demand for creative content, from music and movies to video games and literature. Generating high-quality content traditionally relies heavily on human creativity and labor.

AI Approach

AI-driven systems like OpenAI's GPT-3 can generate text, music, and even visual art. These systems use large-scale neural networks trained on diverse datasets to create new content that mimics human creativity.

Results Achieved

AI-generated content has found applications in various entertainment sectors, from automated news writing to AI-composed music and scriptwriting assistance. While AI has not replaced human creators, it has augmented their capabilities and introduced new forms of interactive media.

Lessons Learned

- Human-AI Collaboration: Combining human creativity with AI capabilities leads to innovative and high-quality content.

- Ethical Considerations: The use of AI in content generation raises questions about authorship, originality, and the potential for abuse.

- Technology Adoption: Ensuring that artists and content creators are comfortable and adept with AI tools is crucial for widespread acceptance.

Case Study 8: Environmental Conservation - Wildlife Monitoring

Overview of the Problem

Monitoring wildlife populations is essential for conservation efforts but is often labor-intensive and challenging, especially in remote or difficult-to-access regions.

AI Approach

AI technologies, including computer vision and machine learning, are deployed to analyze data from camera traps, drones, and satellite imagery. These systems automatically identify and count animal species, track their movements, and monitor their habitats.

Results Achieved

AI-powered wildlife monitoring has dramatically increased the efficiency and accuracy of data collection. For example, researchers used AI to analyze thousands of camera trap images from the Serengeti, identifying and counting animals with high precision.

Lessons Learned

- Scalability: AI enables large-scale monitoring efforts that would be impractical with manual methods.

- Interdisciplinary Collaboration: Success often involves collaboration between AI experts, conservationists, and ecologists.

- Adaptability: AI systems must be adaptable to different environments and species, requiring continuous learning and refinement.

Conclusion

These diverse case studies highlight the transformative impact of AI across various sectors. From healthcare and automotive to finance and entertainment, AI has demonstrated its potential to solve complex problems, enhance efficiency, and drive innovation. The lessons learned from these implementations emphasize the importance of high-quality data, interdisciplinary collaboration, ethical considerations, and the integration of AI with existing practices.

As AI technology continues to evolve, its applications will expand further, presenting new opportunities and challenges. Understanding the practical experiences and outcomes from these case studies provides valuable insights for both current and future endeavors in the field of artificial intelligence.

Chapter 10: Conclusion

Recap of Key Points

As we reach the end of our exploration into the world of Artificial Intelligence, it is essential to reflect on the vast landscape we have traversed. AI is more than just a collection of algorithms and data; it represents a significant leap in humanity's endeavor to understand and replicate intelligence. Let us revisit the essential aspects that define the field of AI.

The Concept of AI

We began by defining AI as the capability of a machine to imitate intelligent human behavior. This broad definition encompasses various aspects such as reasoning, learning, problem-solving, perception, and language understanding. AI emerged from a rich history of human thought and imagination, eventually crystallizing into a formal field of study in the mid-20th century.

Types of AI

We differentiated between Narrow AI (ANI), Artificial General Intelligence (AGI), and Artificial Superintelligence (ASI). Narrow AI systems are specialized and excel in specific domains, such as virtual assistants and recommendation systems. AGI represents a level of machine intelligence that rivals human cognitive abilities across diverse tasks and remains a goal yet to be achieved. ASI, a hypothetical construct, surpasses human intelligence and holds the potential for profound societal impacts.

Fundamental Concepts

Understanding AI requires familiarity with several foundational concepts:

- Machine Learning: The ability of a system to learn from data and improve its performance over time without explicit programming.

- Neural Networks: Inspired by the human brain, these interconnected nodes can process data and recognize patterns.

- Natural Language Processing (NLP): Enables machines to understand, interpret, and generate human language.

- Computer Vision: Allows machines to interpret and make decisions based on visual data.

Core Techniques and Algorithms

We delved into the core techniques and algorithms that power AI systems:

- Supervised Learning: Involves training a model on labeled data, where the outcomes are known, to make future predictions.

- Unsupervised Learning: Deals with unlabeled data, allowing models to identify patterns and groupings within the data.

- Reinforcement Learning: Uses a reward-based system to train agents, optimizing their performance through trial and error.

- Deep Learning: A subset of machine learning that uses multi-layered neural networks to process complex data representations.

Key Technologies and Tools

To implement AI effectively, several technologies and tools are indispensable:

- Programming Languages: Python, R, and Java are commonly used for developing AI applications.

- AI Frameworks: TensorFlow, PyTorch, and Keras simplify the process of building and deploying AI models.

- Data Preparation: Cleaning, transforming, and organizing data are crucial steps for successful AI projects.

AI in Practice

AI has permeated various sectors, revolutionizing how tasks are performed:

- Business and Industry: AI enhances efficiency through automation and intelligent decision-making.

- Healthcare: AI assists in diagnostics, treatment planning, and personalized medicine.

- Autonomous Systems: AI drives advancements in autonomous vehicles, drones, and robotics.

Ethical Considerations and Challenges

The proliferation of AI brings forth several ethical considerations and challenges:

- Bias and Fairness: Mitigating biases in AI systems to ensure fair and equitable outcomes.

- Privacy and Security: Protecting sensitive data and maintaining user privacy.

- Accountability: Ensuring transparency and assigning responsibility for AI-driven decisions.

Future of AI

The future of AI is both promising and uncertain:

- Emerging Trends: Innovations such as quantum computing, neuromorphic engineering, and edge AI are poised to shape the future.

- Predictions: AI's potential to revolutionize various fields, from climate science to personalized education.

- Societal Role: The necessity of integrating AI thoughtfully into society, enhancing human capabilities while addressing ethical concerns.

Getting Started with AI

For those inspired to venture into the field of AI:

- Learning Resources: Various online courses, books, and communities offer valuable knowledge.

- Building First Models: Hands-on practice through projects can consolidate understanding.

- Career Pathways: Opportunities abound in research, development, and application of AI technologies.

Case Studies

Exploring practical implementations of AI provides insights into its potential and limitations:

- Success Stories: AI applications in industries like finance, healthcare, and entertainment.

- Lessons from Failures: Understanding the challenges and avoiding common pitfalls.

- Breakthroughs: Significant innovations that have pushed the boundaries of what AI can achieve.

Final Thoughts on AI's Impact

As we stand on the precipice of an AI-driven future, it is vital to appreciate the transformative potential of this technology. AI is not a singular entity but a collection of methodologies and tools that can augment human capabilities. From automating mundane tasks to solving complex global challenges, AI holds the promise of creating a better world. However, this potential must be harnessed responsibly, with an acute awareness of the ethical considerations and societal implications.

The Ethical Imperative

Ethics in AI is not an afterthought but a central pillar in its development. As we design and deploy intelligent systems, we must prioritize fairness, transparency, and accountability. Addressing biases, ensuring inclusive datasets, and maintaining user privacy are essential steps to prevent harm and build public trust. Regulatory frameworks and interdisciplinary collaboration will play a critical role in shaping an ethical AI landscape.

Interdisciplinary Collaboration

The complexity of AI demands collaboration across disciplines. Computer scientists, ethicists, policymakers, and industry experts must work together to guide the development and deployment of AI systems. Interdisciplinary approaches can help address the multifaceted challenges posed by AI, ensuring that technological advancements align with societal values and norms.

Preparing for the Future

As AI evolves, so must our approach to education and workforce development. Equipping individuals with AI literacy will be crucial in navigating an increasingly AI-integrated world. Educational institutions, governments, and organizations must prioritize training and reskilling programs to prepare people for the jobs of the future.

Embracing Innovation

Innovation is the lifeblood of AI. Encouraging research and fostering a culture of experimentation will drive the field forward. Governments, academia, and private enterprises must invest in research and development to explore new frontiers in AI. Open-source initiatives and collaborative platforms can accelerate progress and democratize access to AI technologies.

Moving Forward with AI Knowledge

As you conclude this journey through the essentials of AI, you are now equipped with a foundational understanding of its concepts, techniques, applications, and ethical considerations. This knowledge serves as a springboard for further exploration, whether you choose to delve deeper into AI research, develop innovative applications, or engage in informed discussions about its societal impact.

Continuous Learning

AI is a dynamic field that evolves rapidly. Staying updated with the latest advancements, research papers, and industry trends is essential. Engaging with AI communities, attending conferences, and participating in workshops can provide valuable insights and networking opportunities.

Practical Application

Applying your AI knowledge to real-world problems is both rewarding and educational. Start with small projects, experiment with different algorithms, and analyze the outcomes. Learning from practical experience will deepen your understanding and enhance your skills.

Informed Advocacy

As an informed individual, you have the power to advocate for responsible AI use. Engage in discussions about AI ethics, contribute to policy-making processes, and promote awareness about the potential and challenges of AI. Informed advocacy ensures that the benefits of AI are realized while mitigating its risks.

Conclusion

"Artificial Intelligence: Only the Essentials" has aimed to provide you with a comprehensive yet concise understanding of AI. From its historical origins to its current applications and future prospects, AI is a field of immense potential and profound impact. As you reflect on what you have learned, remember that AI is not just a technological advancement; it is a tool that, if wielded wisely, can enhance human life and contribute to a better world.

Embrace the knowledge you have gained, continue to explore, and be a part of the journey toward a future where AI serves humanity's highest ideals. The adventure into the realm of intelligent machines is just beginning, and you are now equipped to contribute meaningfully to this exciting frontier. Thank you for embarking on this journey with "Artificial Intelligence: Only the Essentials."

Appendices

Glossary of Terms

Algorithm: A set of rules or steps for solving a problem or performing a task.

Artificial Neural Network (ANN): A computational model inspired by the way biological neural networks in the human brain process information.

Backpropagation: A supervised learning algorithm used for training neural networks, which involves adjusting weights based on the error of the output.

Big Data: Extremely large data sets that can be analyzed computationally to reveal patterns, trends, and associations.

Cognitive Computing: Systems that simulate human thought processes in a computerized model, often using AI to enhance human decision-making.

Convolutional Neural Network (CNN): A type of deep neural network commonly used for analyzing visual data and image recognition.

Data Mining: The practice of examining large databases to generate new information and find hidden patterns.

Deep Learning: A subset of machine learning involving neural networks with many layers, capable of learning from large amounts of data.

Feature Extraction: The process of transforming raw data into a set of features that can be used in machine learning.

Genetic Algorithm: An optimization algorithm inspired by the process of natural selection, used to solve complex problems by evolving a population of candidate solutions.

Internet of Things (IoT): A network of physical objects embedded with sensors, software, and other technologies to exchange data with other devices and systems over the internet.

Machine Learning (ML): A subset of AI where machines improve their performance on tasks by learning from data.

Natural Language Processing (NLP): A field of AI focused on the interaction between computers and humans through natural language.

Overfitting: A modeling error that occurs when a machine learning algorithm performs well on training data but poorly on new, unseen data.

Reinforcement Learning (RL): A type of machine learning where an agent learns to make decisions by performing certain actions and receiving rewards or punishments.

Supervised Learning: A type of machine learning where the model is trained on labeled data, meaning that each training example is paired with an output label.

Support Vector Machine (SVM): A supervised learning algorithm used for classification and regression tasks.

Unsupervised Learning: A type of machine learning where the model is trained on unlabeled data and must find patterns and relationships within the data itself.

Virtual Assistant: An AI-powered software agent that can perform tasks or services for an individual based on commands or questions.

Recommended Reading

"Artificial Intelligence: A Modern Approach" by Stuart Russell and Peter Norvig

This is the most widely used textbook in AI, providing a comprehensive overview of the field.

"Deep Learning" by Ian Goodfellow, Yoshua Bengio, and Aaron Courville

A thorough exploration of deep learning techniques and underlying theories, contributing to the development of the field.

"Superintelligence: Paths, Dangers, Strategies" by Nick Bostrom

An insightful examination of the potential future impacts of superintelligent AI and its associated risks.

"The Master Algorithm" by Pedro Domingos

An engaging introduction to the concept of a single overarching algorithm that could unify all of the existing machine learning paradigms.

"Human Compatible: Artificial Intelligence and the Problem of Control" by Stuart Russell

An investigation into how we can ensure AI systems will remain beneficial and under human control.

"Pattern Recognition and Machine Learning" by Christopher Bishop

A foundational text providing a detailed introduction to machine learning and pattern recognition.

"Thinking, Fast and Slow" by Daniel Kahneman

Though not an AI book in the strict sense, it provides invaluable insights into human decision-making processes, which are crucial for understanding and developing cognitive computing.

"Life 3.0: Being Human in the Age of Artificial Intelligence" by Max Tegmark

A sweeping overview of the implications of AI on our future society and civilization.

Useful Websites and Online Courses

Websites

Artificial Intelligence Index Report (AI Index)

A project by Stanford University providing data to inform AI policy and public debate: [AI Index](https://aiindex.stanford.edu/)

Impact of AI

A comprehensive resource examining the societal implications of AI by the Leverhulme Centre for the Future of Intelligence: [Impact of AI](https://www.leverhulme.ac.uk/our-research/impact-artificial-intelligence)

OpenAI Blog

Regular updates on the latest research and developments from OpenAI: [OpenAI Blog](https://www.openai.com/blog/)

MIT Technology Review – AI

Articles and research discussing the latest trends in AI: [MIT Technology Review - AI](https://www.technologyreview.com/topic/artificial-intelligence/)

Online Courses

Coursera: Machine Learning by Andrew Ng

An excellent introductory course to machine learning, covering various techniques and real-world applications.

edX: Artificial Intelligence by Columbia University

A comprehensive program that delves into the fundamentals and advanced concepts of AI.

Udacity: Deep Learning Nanodegree

A specialized program focusing specifically on deep learning, with hands-on projects to solidify learning.

Khan Academy: Introduction to Algorithms

Provides a strong foundation in algorithms, which are essential for understanding AI.

Fast.ai: Practical Deep Learning for Coders

A hands-on deep learning course designed to teach practical implementation using popular libraries.

MIT OpenCourseWare: Artificial Intelligence

Free access to lecture notes, assignments, and exams from MIT's AI course.

DataCamp: Data Science and Machine Learning

Interactive courses that teach data science and machine learning through exercises and projects.

Further Reading and Resources

Academic Journals

Journal of Artificial Intelligence Research (JAIR)

Publishing papers in all areas of artificial intelligence, focusing on significant developments in the field.

Machine Learning Journal

An international journal publishing scholarly articles on research in machine learning.

Nature Machine Intelligence

A journal covering the broad field of machine learning and artificial intelligence, with an emphasis on the interdisciplinary nature of AI research.

IEEE Transactions on Neural Networks and Learning Systems

Publishing research on the neural networks and learning systems that underpin many AI applications.

Neural Computation

A journal focusing on all aspects of neural computation, from theoretical foundations to applications.

Conferences

NeurIPS (Conference on Neural Information Processing Systems)

One of the most important and prestigious conferences in the field of AI and machine learning.

ICML (International Conference on Machine Learning)

Annual conference highlighting new research across various machine learning domains.

AAAI (Association for the Advancement of Artificial Intelligence) Conference

A major conference covering all aspects of AI research.

IJCAI (International Joint Conference on Artificial Intelligence)

A conference focused on advances and developments in the AI field.

CVPR (Conference on Computer Vision and Pattern Recognition)

A leading event for research in computer vision and pattern recognition.

Libraries and Frameworks

TensorFlow

An open-source machine learning framework developed by Google, highly versatile for building and deploying AI models: [TensorFlow](https://www.tensorflow.org/)

PyTorch

An open-source machine learning library developed by Facebook's AI Research lab for applications such as computer vision and natural language processing: [PyTorch](https://pytorch.org/)

Scikit-learn

A free software machine learning library for Python, providing simple tools for data mining and data analysis: [Scikit-learn](https://scikit-learn.org/)

Keras

A high-level neural networks API, written in Python and capable of running on top of TensorFlow and other frameworks: [Keras](https://keras.io/)

OpenCV

An open-source computer vision and machine learning software library with powerful image processing capabilities: [OpenCV](https://opencv.org/)

NLTK (Natural Language Toolkit)

A leading platform for building Python programs to work with human language data: [NLTK](https://www.nltk.org/)

Strategies for Staying Updated

Newsletters

AI Weekly

A weekly newsletter summarizing the latest in AI research, industry news, and upcoming conferences: [AI Weekly](https://aiweekly.co/)

Import AI

A newsletter edited by Jack Clark from OpenAI, covering key developments in artificial intelligence: [Import AI](https://jack-clark.net/)

Podcasts

The AI Alignment Podcast

A series of discussions on the challenges of ensuring AI systems are aligned with human values.

The TWIML AI Podcast

Interviews and discussions with leaders in the AI and machine learning fields, covering new research, trends, and applications.

The AI Alignment Podcast

A comprehensive series examining AI safety, control, and policy.

Communities

Kaggle

A platform for data science competitions, learning resources, and coding challenges: [Kaggle](https://www.kaggle.com/)

Reddit - Machine Learning

A community for discussing machine learning research, news, and projects: [Reddit Machine Learning](https://www.reddit.com/r/MachineLearning/)

Stack Overflow

A community-driven Q&A site where you can ask questions and share knowledge related to programming and AI: [Stack Overflow](https://stackoverflow.com/)

By exploring these appendices, engaging with the recommended resources, and participating in the suggested communities, you can further deepen your understanding of artificial intelligence. Whether you're a beginner or an advanced practitioner, these resources will provide invaluable insights and knowledge as you continue your journey in the fascinating world of AI.

www.ingramcontent.com/pod-product-compliance
Lightning Source LLC
LaVergne TN
LVHW051716050326
832903LV00032B/4234